STORIES
OF SONGS
ABOUT HEAVEN

STORIES
OF SONGS
ABOUT HEAVEN

by
Ernest K. Emurian

BAKER BOOK HOUSE
Grand Rapids, Michigan

PHOTOLITHOPRINTED BY CUSHING - MALLOY, INC.
ANN ARBOR, MICHIGAN, UNITED STATES OF AMERICA
1972

To

the memory of
my loved ones
who are now at home

in

the house of many mansions

SISTER

BROTHER

MOTHER

FATHER

Preface

This collection begins with the story of the hymn "Heaven Is My Home" and concludes with the history of the hymn "Heaven Is Here," both of which were written by nineteenth century clergymen. The truth of the matter is that to the true Christian heaven is both here and hereafter, our hope as well as our home.

May these simple stories bring strength to the sorrowing, inspiration to the spiritually indifferent, comfort to those in need of consolation, hope to the hopeless, and a vision of glory to all who mourn beside the graves of their loved ones whom they have "loved long since and lost awhile."

A hymn or gospel song may be copyrighted originally for twenty-eight years, renewable, during the last year of the initial copyright, for an additional period of twenty-eight years, or a total of fifty-six years in all. After that time it is in what is known as "Public Domain" (PD) and may be printed or reproduced without written permission and without charge.

All of the selections in this volume have long since gone into "Public Domain" since they were originally copyrighted or renewed more than fifty-six or twenty-eight years ago.

ERNEST K. EMURIAN
Cherrydale United
Methodist Chuch
Arlington, Virginia 22207

CONTENTS

Introduction

Stories of Songs About Heaven contains ten chapters that include such interesting incidents as the remark of the Queen of Sheba to King Solomon that later inspired the sacred song "Not Half Has Ever Been Told"; a message from President McKinley which led a minister to write "Tell Mother I'll Be There"; a singer's dislike of "The Glory Song" which was to become inseparably associated with him in life and in death; a college president's remark that he would not have written "O Think of the Home over There" in his more mature years, although as a young Methodist minister he had felt quite differently about it when his wife died.

Other chapters tell of the death-bed poem of a young British clergyman, "Heaven Is My Home," which was designed to be sung to his favorite tune "Robin Adair"; the music from India for which a Scotsman wrote "Happy Land," which became popular in southern camp meetings; "The Saints' Sweet Home," suggested by Payne's "Home, Sweet Home" and is sung to the same haunting melody; Hart Pease Danks' finest sacred song, "No Night There," which, along with his secular success "Silver Threads Among the Gold," perpetuates his memory today; Mrs. Anne Cousin's stirring stanzas "The Last Words of Samuel Rutherford" from which different stanzas of "The Sands of Time Are Sinking" were selected; and a nineteenth century Universalist minister's one claim to hymnic fame, "Heaven Is Here Where Hymns of Gladness."

The eleventh chapter contains interesting factual notes on twenty other familiar hymns and songs about heaven.

This collection is designed for inspiration as well as instruction, and is, therefore, an ideal gift to present to those who are passing through "the valley of the shadow of death" as well as to the loved ones of those who have already entered "the beautiful city of heaven."

1

Heaven Is My Home

When Carol O'Daly, a handsome young Irish lad from Connaught, "paid his addresses" to Eileen, the "lovely and amiable" daughter of an Irish chieftain from Kavanagh, she returned his affection, but her family and friends strongly disapproved of the romance for political rather than personal reasons, as a consequence of which the youthful swain was forced to flee from Ireland. Eileen's family then soon prevailed upon her to accept the proposal of another suitor, on the ground of her former sweetheart's "supposed unfaithfulness," and the wedding day was set.

However, the evening before the scheduled nuptials, Carol reappeared in the guise of a wandering minstrel. He attended the festivities, mingled with the assembled throng without being recognized, and then was invited to sing. Strumming his guitar, he sang a new love-song which he himself had written and composed during the months of his self-imposed exile, a song entitled "Eileen Aroon." (Eileen is Irish for Helen, while Aroon means "treasure of my heart.") Eileen quickly recognized her lover's voice and replied to his music by singing some spontaneous lines of her own, in which she pledged undying love to the singer. The story goes that Carol and Eileen eloped that very night and, of course, were married and lived happily ever after.

The poem that Carol sang on that occasion was written in 6.4.6.4.6.6.6.4 poetic meter, meaning that there were eight lines in each stanza, the lines having six and four syllables each. Carol may have sung, to his own haunting melody, lines like these:

> Why should we parted be, Eileen Aroon!
> When thy fond heart's with me, Eileen Aroon!
> Come to those golden skies, Bright days for us may rise,
> Oh! dry those tearful eyes, Eileen Aroon!

When the poet Gerald Griffin (1803-1840) versified that romantic tale many years after it had actually happened, he had Carol sing these seven charming stanzas:

> When like the early rose, Eileen Aroon,
> Beauty in childhood blows, Eileen Aroon,
> When, like a diadem, Buds blush around the stem,
> Which is the fairest gem? Eileen Aroon.
>
> Is it the laughing eye, Eileen Aroon,
> Is it the timid sigh, Eileen Aroon,
> Is it the tender tone, Soft as the stringed harp's moan?
> Oh, it is truth alone, Eileen Aroon.
>
> When like the rising day, Eileen Aroon,
> Love sends his early ray, Eileen Aroon,
> What makes his dawning glow Changeless through joy or woe?
> Only the constant know; Eileen Aroon.
>
> I know a valley fair, Eileen Aroon,
> I know a cottage there, Eileen Aroon,
> For in that valley's shade I knew a gentle maid,
> Flower of a hazel glade; Eileen Aroon.
>
> Who in the song so sweet? Eileen Aroon.
> Who in the dance so fleet? Eileen Aroon.
> Dear were her charms to me, Dearer her laughter free,
> Dearest her constancy; Eileen Aroon.

Were she no longer true, Eileen Aroon;
What should her lover do? Eileen Aroon.
Fly with his broken chain Far o'er the bounding main,
Never to love again; Eileen Aroon.

Youth must with time decay, Eileen Aroon;
Beauty must fade away, Eileen Aroon;
Castles are sacked in war, Chieftains are scattered far,
Truth is a fixéd star, Eileen Aroon.

There is a well-founded tradition that this Irish love song was carried across the water to nearby Scotland about 1710 by a blind minstrel named Denis Hempson, and that the Highland singers soon adopted "Eileen Aroon" as their very own. While this beautiful ballad has been dated as early as 1450 and as late as 1625, it is a matter of record that history repeated itself in the eighteenth century in the following manner.

A handsome and quite dashing Irish youth from County Antrim, Robert Adair by name, was in Dublin, Ireland, pursuing the study of medicine when he got into some kind of scrape and was forced to flee for his life. On his way to London, hoping to be able to resume his interrupted studies although penniless, he witnessed an accident in which a carriage was overturned and some of the passengers injured. Offering his services, he assisted in rescuing the passengers and righting their carriage.

One of the recipients of Adair's kindness happened to be a distinguished woman of wealth and culture who immediately invited the thoughtful young man to share the carriage for the duration of the journey. En route they discussed his financial plight and when he reached his destination, his hostess presented him with a generous gift of money for the furtherance of his education, and invited him to visit her home at his convenience.

At a party at that home one night, Robert Adair was

introduced to lovely Lady Caroline Keppel, the second daughter of the Earl of Keppel, and again it was love at first sight. Her kinsfolk were horrified at the prospect of a poor, unknown Irishman taking as his bride the fairest flower of their kingdom, so they forced Caroline to travel abroad and then introduced her to other suitors in a futile attempt to compel her to forget Robert, but all to no avail.

When she was in Bath, England, where she had been sent by a physician who was becoming alarmed at her declining health, Caroline Keppel expressed her feelings in a poem prepared to be sung to the haunting strains of "Eileen Aroon," only this time the girl was singing to the boy and the song was entitled "Robin Adair," Robin being her pet name for Robert. Two of her stanzas tell her story far more eloquently than any prose:

> What's this dull town to me? Robin's not here;
> He whom I wish to see, wish so to hear.
> Where's all the joy and mirth, made life a heaven on earth?
> O! They're all fled with thee, Robin Adair.

> What made th' Assembly shine? Robin Adair.
> What made the ball so fine? Robin Adair.
> What, when the play was o'er, what made my heart so sore?
> O! it was parting with Robin Adair.

When her doctors finally despaired of her life, Caroline's family agreed to let her see her sweetheart, and they were married on February 22, 1758. While Caroline never fully recovered her physical strength, and died after the birth of their third child, Robin lived until his eightieth year. He passed away in 1790 and was laid to rest beside his beloved wife.

"Eileen Aroon" was published as late as 1740 and "Robin Adair" came from the presses just a few years after Robert and Caroline were married. The lovely melody became a favorite of Irishmen, Scotchmen, and Englishmen as well, being used by many composers in a wide variety of ways. Thus it came to pass, that, when the twenty-eight-year-old British Congregational minister Rev. Thomas Rawson Taylor (1807-1835) lay dying, his thoughts turned simultaneously to the promised prospects of heaven and the lilting strains of the popular ballad "Robin Adair." Whether anyone else had ever tried writing sacred stanzas for that secular music has not been determined, but Taylor felt inspired to try his hand at it as he lay on his deathbed.

The son of a Congregational clergyman, Thomas Rawson Taylor was born at Ossett, near Wakefield, England, May 9, 1897, and educated at the Free School in Bradford and Leaf Square Academy, Manchester. After working for two years with a merchant and a printer, he decided, at the age of eighteen, to prepare for the Christian ministry, and entered Airedale Independent College. His only pastoral charge was Howard Street Chapel in Sheffield, which he served for just six months, from July 1830 to January 1831. During that time he was also a tutor at his alma mater, Airedale College. When his health failed, he was forced to resign both positions, and, after an illness of several months, he died on March 7, 1835. It was during those early March days that he penned his hymn on heaven:

> I'm but a stranger here, Heaven is my home;
> Earth is a desert drear, Heaven is my home.
> Dangers and sorrows stand round me on every hand,
> Heaven is my fatherland, Heaven is my home.
>
> What though the tempest rage, Heaven is my home;
> Short is my pilgrimage, Heaven is my home.
> And time's wild wintry blast soon will be overpast;
> I shall reach home at last, Heaven is my home.

Peace! O my troubled soul, Heaven is my home;
I soon shall reach the goal, Heaven is my home;
Swiftly the race I'll run, yield up my crown to none,
Forward! the prize is won, Heaven is my home.

Therefore I murmur not, Heaven is my home;
Whate'er my earthly lot, Heaven is my home.
And I shall surely stand there at my Lord's right hand;
Heaven is my fatherland, Heaven is my home.

There at my Saviour's side, Heaven is my home;
I shall be glorified, Heaven is my home.
There are the good and blest; those I love most and best;
There, too, I soon shall rest, Heaven is my home.

In 1836, the year after Taylor's untimely death, his friend W. S. Matthews published his "Memoirs and Select Remains." This particular poem bears the caption "Heaven Is My Home . . . Air 'Robin Adair.'" Later, editors wedded Taylor's words with the tune "St. Edmund," which the talented British composer Sir Arthur Sullivan had written in 1872, and it is generally in this form that the hymn appears today. So, in three different centuries and in three different countries, poets and composers unwittingly collaborated to give Christendom this hymn on heaven.

While the love stories of Carol and Eileen and Robin and Caroline will be told and retold for many centuries, the story of God's love for His children in every place and in every age will continue to be told and retold for countless generations until earth becomes like heaven in fulfillment of the promise given to us by Christ our Lord when He taught us to pray, "Thy kingdom come . . . on earth as it is in heaven." Whereas, in some cases, the knowledge of divine love becomes the inspiration for human love, in these instances human love became the instrument for the expression of divine love.

HEAVEN IS MY HOME

Scotch Melody.

mf Adagio e Legato.

1. { I'm but a stranger here, Heav'n is my home; }
   { Earth is a desert drear, Heav'n is my home; } Danger and sorrow stand
2. { What tho' the tempest rage? Heav'n is my home; }
   { Short is my pil-grimage, Heav'n is my home; } [blast
                                                    Time's cold and wintry

Round me on ev-'ry hand; Heav'n is my Fatherland, Heav'n is my home.
Soon will be o-ver-past; I shall reach home at last; Heav'n is my home.

3 Peace! O my troubled soul,
  Heav'n is my home;
I soon shall reach the goal,
  Heav'n is my home;
Swiftly the race I'll run,
Yield up my crown to none,
Forward! the prize is won,
  Heav'n is my home.

4 There, at my Saviour's side,
  Heav'n is my home;
I shall be glorified,
  Heav'n is my home:
There are the good and blest,
Those I loved most and best,
There, too, I soon shall rest,
  Heav'n is my home.

This hymn, to the tune "Oak," composed by the father of American church and public school music, Dr. Lowell Mason (1792-1872), is found in *Hymns of the Ages,* by Robert Kerr, published in New York City in 1891 by the A. D. F. Randolph Company, Hymn 613. Arranged to be sung to

Sullivan's tune "St. Edmund," this is Hymn 639 in the 1918 printing of the 1911 edition of *The Hymnal* of the Presbyterian Church in the USA, published in Philadelphia.

The song "Robin Adair" is included in *The Golden Book of Favorite Songs*, published by the Hall and McCreary Company, Chicago, page 39, where it is called "Scotch Air." It is also found on page 83 of *Favorite Songs of the People*, a publication of the Theodore Presser Company, Bryn Mawr, Pennsylvania, 1927, where the music is also given a Scotch rather than an Irish origin.

2

Immanuel's Land
(The Sands of Time Are Sinking)

Two hundred years after the death of the Scottish divine Rev. Samuel Rutherford (1600-1661), a fellow Scot, Mrs. Anne Ross Cousin, took the clergyman's dying words and fashioned them into her most effective, most popular, and most powerful poem.

Rutherford was a remarkable, nonconforming clergyman whose ecclesiastical ups and downs reflected and mirrored the trying days when the Covenanters of Scotland were struggling with the Anglican rulers of England, especially those British kings who demanded complete control over the religious lives of their Caledonian subjects to the north. Dreading the domination of an Anglican monarch as much as they had once feared the dictatorship of an Italian pontiff, the Scottish people refused to submit, and wrote into church history one of her noblest, as well as one of her bloodiest, chapters.

A native of Nisbet, Roxburghshire, Scotland, where he was born the opening year of the seventeenth century, Rutherford graduated from the famed University of Edinburgh, and then served his alma mater as the Professor of Humanity for several years after being awarded his master's degree. The call of the Christian ministry, however, was so strong and insistent that, after teaching for four years, he entered the theological seminary to prepare himself for service in a Protestant parish. When his seminary training was completed, he was ordained and settled down in the west coast town of Anworth where he was destined to become the town's beloved "able and impressive minister."

The temper of the times is reflected in the fact that just twenty-four years after Rutherford's death in 1661, the Wigton Martyrs gave up their lives, their martyrdom taking place at Solway Firth in the waters of Blednoch on May 11, 1685. Two Christian Covenanter women, Margaret Wilson, sixteen, and Margaret McLaughlin, sixty, were tied to stakes at low tide and left there to drown for refusing to "renounce the Covenant" upon orders of the king and his magistrate. It was of the Anworth period in Rutherford's life that Mrs. Cousin wrote in her stirring stanzas two centuries later when she included these lines in her masterpiece, "The Last Words of Samuel Rutherford":

> E'en Anworth was not heaven, e'en preaching was not Christ,
> And in my sea-beat prison my Lord and I held tryst;
> And, aye, my murkiest storm cloud was by a rainbow spanned,
> Caught from the glory dwelling in Immanuel's land.
>
> The little birds at Anworth, I used to count them blest;
> Now beside happier altars I go to build my nest;
> O'er these there broods no silence, no graves around them stand,
> For glory, deathless, dwelleth in Immanuel's land.
>
> Fair Anworth by the Solway, to me thou still art dear;
> E'en from the verge of heaven I drop for thee a tear;
> Oh, if one soul from Anworth meet me at God's right hand,
> My heaven will be two heavens in Immanuel's land.

But the calmness of this rural retreat was soon shattered. A professorship was offered Rutherford on the continent of Europe because of a brilliant theological treatise recently published by the country pastor, so he moved across the channel to Utrecht. But notice sometimes brings notoriety in its wake, and soon Rutherford was summoned back home for his flagrant nonconformity to the acts of the Episcopacy in Scotland, and brought to public trial on July 27, 1636, for his open defiance of the orders of the king. Deprived of his Anworth parish, he was then banished to Aberdeen, but soon the Covenanters once again "gained the ascendancy" and back to the familiar scenes of Anworth the beleaguered clergyman traced his itinerant steps.

There followed in rapid succession another eminent professorship, this time at St. Andrew's, and Rutherford became one of the distinguished divines who constituted the historic Westminster Assembly which prepared the Reformed and Presbyterian Confession of Faith and Catechisms which survive to this very day. Four more volumes came from his pen during these productive and busy years, but the Restoration of 1660 again found him under the regal ban, deprived once more of all of his pastoral and professorial offices and summoned before Parliament to answer charges of "high treason," which is merely "heresy in disguise." The dying prisoner sent his accusers this statement:

"I am summoned before a higher court and judicatory; the first summons I behoove to answer; and ere a few days arrive, I shall be where few kings and great folks come."

A short while before his death on March 20, 1661, Rutherford had a vision of heaven and cried out:

"Oh, that all my brethren may know what a Master

I have served and what peace I have this day. I shall sleep in Christ and when I awake, I shall be satisfied in his likeness. This night shall close the door and put my anchor within the veil, and I shall go to sleep by five o'clock in the morning. Glory, glory to my Creator and my Redeemer forever. I shall live and adore him. Oh, for arms to embrace him. Oh, for a well-tuned harp. Glory, glory dwelleth in Immanuel's land!"

Although this true story was told and retold for two hundred years throughout the length and breadth of nonconforming Scotland, especially among the Presbyterians and Covenanters, it was not until Mrs. Cousin came upon the scene that anyone had successfully attempted to put that vision into poetic or hymnic form. The poet herself was the daughter of a clergyman, Dr. David Ross Cundell of Leith, and the wife of Rev. William Cousin, one-time minister of the Free Church in Melrose, Scotland.

This gifted woman was so moved by the story of the life and death of the famed hero, particularly his dying words, "Glory, glory dwelleth in Immanuel's land," that sometime about the year 1857 she began to weave them into a new poem, a composition that grew and grew until she had penned nineteen eight-line stanzas, too long for a hymn and yet too little for a book. In her brief epic, Mrs. Cousin told of the life, ministry, suffering, and triumphant death of Rev. Samuel Rutherford, little dreaming that one day several of her stanzas would be taken out of their context to become one of the finest hymns on heaven and immortality ever penned by a devout Christian woman. In one group of these stanzas, the author has the clergyman say:

Oh, Christ, he is the fountain, the deep, sweet well of love;
The streams on earth I've tasted, more deep I'll drink above;

24

> There to an ocean fullness, his mercy doth expand,
> And glory, glory dwelleth in Immanuel's land.

> The bride eyes not her garment but her dear
>   bridegroom's face;
> I will not gaze at glory but on my King of Grace—
> Not at the crown he giveth, but on his piercéd hand;
> The Lamb is all the glory of Immanuel's land.

"Immanuel" she knew was one of the prophetic names ascribed to Jesus and means "God with us" (Matthew 1:23, quoted from Isaiah 7:14). In the stanza that eventually began her noblest hymn, Anne Ross Cousin (1824-1906) continued the same thought woven into a varied pattern, as she wrote:

> The sands of time are sinking; the dawn of heaven breaks;
> The summer morn I've sighed for, the fair, sweet
>   morn awakes.
> Dark, dark hath been the midnight, but dayspring is at hand,
> And glory, glory dwelleth in Immanuel's land.

When the 1894 edition of *Gospel Hymns One to Six Complete,* a Moody and Sankey publication, came from the press, three stanzas of "Immanuel's Land" were included in two different places, attesting to the popularity of the hymn among American Christians. Hymn 67 dates Mrs. Cousin's poem as 1857, and is arranged to be sung to a tune by C. M. Wyman, while the same three stanzas are included as Hymn 252, to be sung to an original tune by Ira D. Sankey himself. Sixty years later, when the 1954 printing of *The Methodist Hymnal* was prepared for British Methodists, four stanzas of Mrs. Cousin's poem were included, to be sung to a tune named "Rutherford," composed in Paris in 1834 by the French composer Chrétien Urhan (1790-1845), revealing the high favor in which the Scottish poet's stanzas were held by English Methodists a hundred years after their composition.

It is interesting to note that the Sankey version and the British *Methodist Hymn Book* version are similar only in the fact that they begin with "The sands of time are sinking" as the first stanza. Sankey selected two others from Mrs. Cousin's original nineteen, while the Methodist editors chose three entirely different stanzas for their publication.

The poet herself closed her brilliant versified biography of one of her country's stalwart saints with these majestic stanzas in which she portrayed the persecuted spiritual patriot affirming his faith in the assurance of immortality:

> I've wrestled on toward heaven 'gainst storm and
>   wind and tide;
> Now like a weary traveller that leaneth on his guide
> Amid the shades of evening, while sinks life's
>   lingering sand,
> I hail the glory dawning from Immanuel's land.
>
> Deep waters crossed life's pathway, the hedge
>   of thorns was sharp;
> Now these all lie behind me; O, for a well-tuned harp!
> O to join the hallelujah with yon triumphant band,
> Who sing where glory dwelleth in Immanuel's land.
>
> The King there in his beauty without a veil is seen;
> It were a well-spent journey though seven deaths
>   lay between.
> The Lamb with his fair army doth on Mount Zion stand;
> And glory, glory dwelleth in Immanuel's land.
>
> Oh, I am my Beloved's and my Beloved's mine;
> He brings a poor, vile sinner into his "house of wine";
> I stand upon his merit, I know no other stand;
> Not e'en where glory dwelleth in Immanuel's land.

With mercy and with judgment my web of time he wove;
And aye the dews of sorrow were lustered by his love.
I'll bless the hand that guided, I'll bless the heart
    that planned,
When throned where glory dwelleth in Immanuel's land.

Oh, well it is forever; Oh, well, forevermore;
My nest hung in no forest of all this death-doomed shore;
Yea, let this vain world vanish, as from the ship the strand,
While glory, glory dwelleth in Immanuel's land.

I have borne scorn and hatred, I have borne
    wrong and shame;
Earth's proud ones have reproached me for Christ's
    thrice blesséd name;
Where God's seals set the fairest, they've stamped
    their foulest brand;
But judgment shines like noonday in Immanuel's land.

They've summoned me before them, but there I
    may not come;
My Lord says "Come up hither"; my Lord says
    "Welcome home."
My King at his white throne room my presence
    doth command,
Where glory, glory dwelleth in Immanuel's land.

Since these stanzas are written in 7.6.7.6.D. poetic meter, alternating lines having seven and six syllables each, with the pattern of four lines being doubled into eight-line stanzas, they may be sung to such familiar hymn tunes as "Aurelia" ("The Church's One Foundation"); "Lancashire" ("Lead On, O King Eternal"); and "Webb" ("Stand Up, Stand Up For Jesus," or "The Morning Light Is Breaking"). Four stanzas arranged to be sung to the tune "Rutherford" may be found in the 1918 printing of the 1911 edition of *The Hymnal,* published by The Presbyterian Church in the USA in Philadelphia, Hymn 629.

THE SANDS OF TIME ARE SINKING

RUTHERFORD

Anne Ross Cousin

Christian Urhan
Arr. by Edward F. Rimbault

1. The sands of time are sink - ing, The dawn of heav - en breaks;
2. O Christ, He is the foun - tain, The deep, sweet well of love!
3. With mer - cy and with judg - ment My web of time He wove,

The sum - mer morn I've sighed for, The fair, sweet morn, a - wakes;
The streams on earth I've tast - ed More deep I'll drink a - bove:
And aye the dews of sor - row Were lus - tered by His love.

Dark, dark hath been the mid - night, But day - spring is at hand,
There to an o - cean full - ness His mer - cy doth ex - pand,
I'll bless the hand that guid - ed, I'll bless the heart that planned,

And glo - ry, glo - ry dwell - eth In Im - man - uel's land.
And glo - ry, glo - ry dwell - eth In Im - man - uel's land.
When throned where glo - ry dwell - eth In Im - man - uel's land. A-MEN.

29

3

No Night There

Irish-born John R. Clements (1868-1946) began to write original verses when he was fifteen "because," he said, "I could not help it!" But he was honest enough to admit that his fellowship with Christian people gave him the inspiration he needed, especially in the youth activities in which they were engaged. "Christian Endeavour put the devotional touch to my pen," he confessed, and it came as no surprise to him or his coworkers that, prior to his death at the age of seventy-eight, he penned more hymns and edited more song books than any other person associated with the Christian Endeavour movement in the United States.

Born in County Armagh, Ireland, November 28, 1868, John was brought by his parents to the United States when he was only two years old. He received his early education in a typical rural "little red school house" and began working when he was thirteen, beginning as a clerk in a grocery store and advancing through the years until he became a successful wholesale grocery-man in Binghamton, New York, the city in which he spent most of the years of his long, active, and creative life.

When the lay evangelist Dwight Lyman Moody held a series of revival services in Binghamton's First Presbyterian Church in 1886, eighteen-year-old John Clements was one of his first converts, and for the next sixty years he was an active member of that congregation, serving as a teacher and as a deacon, and in other lay capacities as well. His close connection with the growing youth movement enabled him to develop in the Christian life, and he always remained aware of the opportunities which this fellowship had afforded him. "I was discovered, developed, and educated by, through, and in Christian Endeavour," he said proudly. The group rewarded him by electing him state president and inviting him to address several international conventions.

When John's first poem was accepted for publication in a New York State farm journal, the young lad was encouraged to continue expressing himself in poems and verses. His first successful song, "Man the Life Boat," was written when he was just seventeen. More than three thousand more songs were to come from his prolific pen before he was translated to the Church triumphant, among them the perenniel favorites "Somebody Did a Golden Deed" (music by W. S. Weeden in 1901), "Just a Little Sunshine," and "No Night There."

He received the inspiration for his popular hymn on heaven while reading through the last two chapters of the last book of the Bible, the Revelation of St. John, chapters twenty-one and twenty-two. Several phrases that the Beloved Apostle used in describing the New Jerusalem caught his eye, among them such familiar words as these: "And the gates of it shall not be shut at all by day; for there shall be no night there" (21:25); "and the city lieth foursquare" (21:16); "and the city was pure gold" (21:18); "every several gate was of one pearl"

(21:21); "and God shall wipe away all tears from their eyes, and there shall be no more death, neither sorrow nor crying" (21:4). In a very short while, the devout Presbyterian layman was writing down his new stanzas based upon those very words from Scripture:

1. In the land of fadeless day Lies the "city foursquare,"
   It shall never pass away And there is "no night there."

CHORUS: God shall "wipe away all tears"; There's no
   death, no pain nor fears;
        And they count not time by years, For there
        is "no night there."

2. All the gates of pearl are made, In the "city foursquare,"
   All the streets with gold are laid, And there is
        "no night there."

3. And the gates shall never close, To the "city foursquare,"
   There life's crystal river flows, And there is
        "no night there."

4. There they need no sunshine bright, In that
        "city foursquare,"
   For the Lamb is all the light, And there is
        "no night there."

Although D. B. Towner ("Trust and Obey"), Elisha Hoffman ("Leaning on the Everlasting Arms"), and Charles Gabriel ("The Awakening Chorus") had composed wonderful tunes for many of Clements' stanzas, the poet sent these particular stanzas to his publisher, who immediately forwarded them to Hart Pease Danks (1834-1903), requesting him to compose an appropriate tune. Danks, a native of New Haven, Connecticut, where he was born April 6, 1834, had studied music at Saratoga Springs, New York, with Dr. L. E. Whiting, moving later to Chicago where he became a professional photographer as well as a successful choir director, entertainer, and bass soloist.

Danks married Hattie R. Colahan of Cleveland, Ohio, January 25, 1858, and six years later moved with his wife and three children to New York City, to devote all of his time to music. His first popular song, "De Cabin on De Mississippi Shore," was Stephen Foster-ish in style but not in its widespread use or its pecuniary reward, and it was not until 1873 that he reached the zenith of his creative powers when he set Wisconsin editor Eben Rexford's poem "Silver Threads Among the Gold" to beautiful music, a song that became an instantaneous success, selling more than two million copies within a very few years.

Danks' total musical output was in excess of thirteen hundred separate compositions, among them two operettas, "Pauline, or The Belle of Saratoga," published in 1872, and "Conquered by Kindness" in 1881; a sacred song, "Not Ashamed of Christ," in 1873; and a musical sequel to "Silver Threads," a sentimental song entitled "Don't Be Angry with Me, Darling." But only his musical settings for John Clement's sacred song "No Night There" and Eben Rexford's sentimental song "Silver Threads Among the Gold" perpetuate his memory today. Many of his anthems were widely used throughout the country during the composer's lifetime, several being included in William Bradbury's famous "Jubilee Collection."

Tragically enough, Hart Pease Danks and his wife separated in 1898, and the songwriter moved to Philadelphia where he made his residence in a cheap rooming house at 1210 Race Street. It was there on the morning of November 20, 1903, his sixty-ninth year, that his landlady, Mrs. Maud Hartman, found him kneeling by his bed, stiff and cold in death. When his body was lifted from its awkward position by police officers, they discovered that the deceased musician's face had been resting on a piece of popular music entitled "Silver Threads Among the Gold." In his fingers, the dead man still clutched the stub of a pencil with which he had written these final words across the attractive cover of the song that had brought him fame and fortune, "It's hard to grow old alone." Twenty years later, his widow died in Brooklyn, New York.

> Somebody did a golden deed,
> Proving himself a friend in need;
> Somebody sang a cheerful song,
> Brightening the sky the whole day long—
> Was that somebody you?
> Was that somebody you?

The words and music of "No Night There" may be found in many hymnals and song books; it is 419 in the 1944 edition of *The Service Hymnal,* Hope Publishing Company, Chicago, Illinois.

NO NIGHT THERE

John R. Clements

Hart P. Danks

1. In the land of fade-less day Lies the "cit-y four-square,"
2. All the gates of pearl are made, In the "cit-y four-square,"
3. And the gates shall nev-er close To the "cit-y four-square,"
4. There they need no sun-shine bright, In that "cit-y four-square,"

It shall nev-er pass a-way, And there is "no night there."
All the streets with gold are laid, And there is "no night there."
There life's crys-tal riv-er flows, And there is "no night there."
For the Lamb is all the light, And there is "no night there."

CHORUS

mf

God shall "wipe a-way all tears;" There's no death, no pain, nor fears;
God shall "wipe a-way all tears;" There's no death, no pain, nor fears;

f   *dim.*   *mf*

And they count not time by years, For there is "no night there."
And they count not time by years, by years, For there is "no night... there."

4

Not Half Has Ever Been Told

The inspiration for this hymn on heaven was a Biblical phrase taken from the Queen of Sheba's comment on the wisdom of King Solomon, a statement that was later coupled with some of the picturesque imagery from the Revelation of John that resulted in the plaintive gospel song that began with this stanza and chorus:

> 1. I have read of a beautiful city
>   Far away in the kingdom of God.
>   I have read how its walls are of jasper,
>   How its streets are all golden and broad;
>   In the midst of the street is life's river,
>   Clear as crystal and pure to behold,
>   But not half of that city's bright glory
>   To mortals has ever been told.
> CHORUS: Not half has ever been told,
>   Not half has ever been told;
>   Not half of that city's bright glory
>   To mortals has ever been told.

Of course, the words "jasper walls" and "golden streets" are taken directly from the last book in the Bible, but none of the New Testament writers coined the phrase "not half has ever been told." Those words appear in the Old Testament for the first time in I Kings 10:7, in the tribute paid by Sheba to Solomon which contained, in part, this testimony from the Queen of the South, "Howbeit I believed not the words until I came and mine eyes have seen; and, behold, the half was not told me; thy wisdom and prosperity exceedeth the fame which I heard."

An American Methodist minister, Rev. Jonathan Bush Atchinson (1840-1882), during his thirty-fifth year, coupled the tribute of Sheba with some of the promises of Jesus and portions of John's Revelation and made the African ruler's words apply not to Solomon's earthly kingdom but to God's heavenly kingdom. Atchinson, a native of Wilson, New York, where he was born on February 18, 1840, penned his descriptive lines in 1875, his second, third, and fourth stanzas containing these words:

2. I have read of bright mansions in heaven,
   Which the Saviour has gone to prepare;
And the saints who on earth have been faithful
   Rest forever with Christ over there.
There no sin ever enters, nor sorrow;
   The inhabitants never grow old;
But not half of the joys that await them
   To mortals has ever been told.

3. I have read of white robes for the righteous,
   Of bright crowns which the glorified wear;
When our Father shall bid them, "Come, enter,
   And my glory eternally share."
How the righteous are evermore blessed,
   As they walk through the streets of pure gold;
But not half of the wonderful story
   To mortals has ever been told.

4. I have read of a Christ so forgiving,
   That vile sinners may ask and receive
Peace and pardon for every transgression,
   If when asking they only believe.

> I have read how He'll guide and protect us,
> If for safety we enter His fold;
> But not half of His goodness and mercy
> To mortals has ever been told.

Atchinson's stanzas eventually came to the attention of a fellow New Yorker, fifty-seven-year-old country doctor Otis F. Presbrey (1820-1910) who had been born in York, Livingston County, on December 20, 1820. Presbrey graduated from the Berkshire Medical College in 1847 and entered upon his career as a physician, but his interest in and love for music later led him to devote all of his time and talent to compiling, composing, and editing collections of hymns and sacred songs for many different publishers. The doctor composed the melody for the preacher's poem on heaven in 1877; the full accompaniment was later edited and arranged for publication by a blind musician from Washington, D.C., J. W. Bischoff. Later the composer-editor and another preacher-poet, Rev. J. E. Rankin of "God Be with You till We Meet Again" fame, collaborated on an 1883 publication entitled "Gospel Bells."

Atchinson was so pleased with the response to his hymn on heaven that he was inspired to create another and then still another, writing such well-known gospel songs as "There's a Stranger at the Door, Let Him In," for which the popular song-leader and composer Edwin O. Excell (1851-1921) composed the music, as he did again in 1881 for another Atchinson poem, "In the Shadow of His Wings There Is Rest, Rest, Rest."

The emotional appeal which greeted the singing of "Not Half Has Ever Been Told" as a sacred solo by Ira D. Sankey is vouched for by several dramatic stories which Mr. Sankey included in his autobiography which was first published in 1906, several years after poet Atchinson had entered "the beautiful city of heaven."

Well-known American gospel singer, arranger, and composer Ralph E. Hudson (1834-1901) came into the musical arena at the time when the Sunday school movement was just getting under way and he felt the need to compose new tunes for several of the great hymns of the faith, so that the children and young people who were then flocking to the churches in larger and larger numbers could learn them quickly and use them regularly.

With that in mind, in 1885 Mr. Hudson took Rev. Isaac Watts' poetic masterpiece, "Alas and Did My Saviour Bleed," first published in 1719, composed a lilting tune for those lines to supplant the dignified and stately cadences of the hymn tune "Martyrdom, Avon," added a chorus that would have made Dr. Watts "turn over in his grave," and soon had everyone singing "At the Cross," which was merely Watts as edited, emended, and supplemented by Hudson.

Encouraged by that initial effort, Hudson went a step further and decided to do the same thing with a hymn from the fluent pen of Britain's renowned woman poet Frances Ridley Havergal (1836-1879). This hymn began with this common meter stanza:

> 1. I know I love Thee better, Lord, Than any earthly joy;
> For thou hast given me the peace Which nothing
> can destroy.

Hudson composed another lilting tune for those lines, again added a chorus all his very own, taken directly from the Atchinson-Presbrey success of a few years earlier, and soon had everyone singing this chorus, which came from his own creative imagination and not from that of the poetic purist Miss Havergal:

> The half has never yet been told, Of love so full and free;
> The half has never yet been told, The blood it
> cleanseth me.

So popular did this simple chorus of Hudson's become that Miss Havergal's hymn has been known since then as "The Half Has Never Yet Been Told" instead of "I Know I Love Thee Better, Lord," although it is highly doubtful that she ever used that phrase in any of the dozens of superb hymns she wrote during her brief life of forty-three years, among them such hymnic gems as "True Hearted, Whole Hearted," "Lord, Speak to Me, That I May Speak," "Another Year Is Dawning," and "Take My Life and Let It Be." More than likely the stanzas of this particular hymn would never have become as popular as they are today had not Mr. Hudson come upon the scene with his determination to popularize the hymns of yesterday in order to make them more attractive to the Sunday school scholars of his own day. Be that as it may, to this day Miss Havergal is poetically wedded to Mr. Hudson, and these lines are still being sung to his familiar music:

> 2. I know that Thou art nearer still Than any earthly throng;
> And sweeter is the thought of Thee Than any lovely song.

> 3. Thou hast put gladness in my heart; Then well
> may I be glad;
> Without the secret of Thy love I could not but be sad.

> 4. O Saviour, precious Saviour mine! What will Thy
> presence be,
> If such a life of joy can crown Our walk on
> earth with Thee.

The Queen of Sheba had not the remotest idea that what she said to King Solomon at the close of their historic visit would one day be linked inseparably with some of the comforting words of the Saviour and the vision of the Apostolic Seer; yet her phrase has been aptly utilized, for truly "eye hath not seen, nor ear heard, neither have entered into the heart of man the things which God hath prepared for them that love him" (I Corinthians 2:9). As each stanza of this hymn-poem states, no one, not even the most devout and dedicated Christian, can have but the vaguest idea of the glory of God's Kingdom that exists on the other side of death. Truly, "not half has ever been told."

The words and music of "Not Half Has Ever Been Told," arranged as a sacred solo, may be found in *The Cokesbury Worship Hymnal,* 1938 edition, published by The Methodist Publishing House (Cokesbury Press), Nashville, Tennessee, Hymn 276.

Miss Frances Havergal's hymn, with Mr. Hudson's tune, may be found in *Life and Service Hymns,* published in 1917 by The Presbyterian Publication Board, Richmond, Virginia, Hymn 21. In this book the hymn is entitled "I Know I Love Thee Better, Lord." In the *Hymnal of the Church of God,* published in 1953 by the Gospel Trumpet Company, Anderson, Indiana, it is Hymn 272, entitled "The Half Has Never Been Told."

NOT HALF HAS EVER BEEN TOLD

JOHN BURCH ATCHINSON

O. F. PRESBREY

1. I have read of a beau - ti - ful cit - y, Far a-
2. I have read of bright man - sions in heav - en, Which the
3. I have read of white robes for the right - eous, Of bright
4. I have read of a Christ so for - giv - ing, That vile

way in the king-dom of God; I have read how its walls are of
Sav - ior has gone to pre - pare; And the saints who on earth have been
crowns which the glo - ri - fied wear, When our Fa - ther shall bid them "Come,
sin - ners may ask and re - ceive Peace and par - don for ev - 'ry trans-

jas - per, How its streets are all gold - en and broad: In the
faith - ful, Rest for - ev - er with Christ o - ver there; There no
en - ter, And My glo - ry e - ter - nal - ly share;" How the
gres - sion, If when ask - ing they on - ly be - lieve. I have

42

midst of the street is life's riv - er, Clear as crys - tal and pure to be-
sin   ev - er en - ters, nor sor - row, The in - hab - it - ants nev - er grow
right-eous are ev - er-more bless - ed   As they walk thro' the streets of pure
read how He'll guide and pro-tect us, If   for safe - ty we en - ter His

hold,   But not half of that city's bright glory To mortals has ev-er been told.
old;   But not half of the wonderful sto - ry To mortals has ev-er been told.
gold;   But not half of the wonderful sto - ry To mortals has ev-er been told.
fold;   But not half of His goodness and mercy To mortals has ev-er been told.

REFRAIN

Not half has ev - er been told;.. Not half has ev - er been told;.. Not
                     been told;   been told;

Repeat the Refrain p

half of that cit - y's bright glo - ry To mor-tals has ev - er been told.

5

O Think of the Home over There

Many years after his gospel song about heaven had carried its message of hope around the Christian world, someone asked the preacher-poet Rev. DeWitt Clinton Huntington (1830-1912), "If you had it to do over again, would you write the sacred stanzas of 'The Home over There' as you did when you first penned those lines back in 1866?" The distinguished clergyman-turned-educator replied, "I don't think I would, because I have since discovered that there is so much to be done here and now that we should not think too much about the future."

Despite that frank confession, however, the young Methodist minister had felt quite differently about it when he lost his first wife while he was serving as pastor of the Frank Street Methodist Church in Rochester, New York.

Huntington, the son of a learned and honored New England circuit judge and a devout and "distinctly determined Puritan mother," was born in Townsend, Vermont, April 27, 1830. In spite of a remarkable religious awakening that came over him when, as a lad of five, he heard his mother pray one morning, he decided to follow his father's profession and take up the study of law.

During his seventeenth year he experienced what he called "conversion" under the evangelistic preaching of Rev. Moses Spencer, united with the church, turned his back upon a promising legal career, and embraced the Methodist ministry. His sister said of him, after DeWitt became chancellor of Nebraska Wesleyan University, Lincoln, Nebraska, "A good boy developed into an educated man by untiring industry, great energy, and rigid economy." After he answered the call to the Christian ministry, the young convert said, "From the time I was ten years old I knew the Lord was in my life. In the morning when I went after the cows on my father's farm, I used to pray the whole mile, and at night I prayed all the way home. My life has been in His keeping. It has been jagged; my service has been bungling, but I have never taken back the surrender I made."

In the spring of 1849 the Methodist Church licensed Huntington as an "exhorter," giving him his local preacher's license two months later. After teaching school for two years and preaching on Sunday in several local churches, DeWitt rejected an offer of a teaching position at $1,000 a year to receive an appointment to a Methodist church at a salary of only $200 a year. He joined the Vermont Conference in 1851 and was transferred to the East Genesee Conference in New York State six years later. Prior to that transfer, he had served congregations in Thedford, Proctorsville, and Brattleboro, Vermont. Subsequently he was appointed to serve Methodist congregations at Hornellsville, Trumansburg, and Rochester, New York. He was so popular in Rochester that he served in that city on five different occasions, returning to a former charge, Asbury Church, after an absence of sixteen years.

In 1853 Huntington and Miss Mary E. Moore of Chelsea, Vermont, were married and to their union two sons, Thomas and Horace, were born. It was during his pastorate at Rochester's Frank Street Methodist Church that Mrs. Huntington passed away. While the clergyman had not yet cultivated those literary talents that were to be developed in his more mature years, he was so deeply moved by the sense of loss that followed his wife's death that he attempted to resolve part of his spiritual conflict by reducing his emotions and feelings to poetic form. Soon, without too much conscious effort on his part, he wrote four simple stanzas that contained these lines:

1. O think of the home over there,
       By the side of the river of light,
   Where the saints all immortal and fair
       Are robed in their garments of white.

2. O think of the friends over there,
       Who before us the journey have trod,
   Of the songs that they breathe on the air
       In their home in the palace of God.

3. My Saviour is now over there,
       There my kindred and friends are at rest;
   Then away from my sorrow and care,
       Let me fly to the land of the blest.

4. I'll soon be at home over there,
       For the end of my journey I see;
   Many dear to my heart over there
       Are watching and waiting for me.

An Ohio-born musician, composer, one-time professor at Ohio Wesleyan University, and part-time salesman of musical instruments, Tullius Clinton O'Kane (1830-1912), was born the same year as the Methodist preacher-poet. He set the preacher's lines to music, adding a chorus all his own, just as he had done when he added "We will

46

rest in that fair and happy land" to Samuel Stennett's hymn "On Jordan's Stormy Banks I Stand." (It was composer R. M. McIntosh who added the chorus "I'm Bound for the Promised Land" to Stennett's stanzas.) O'Kane added the words "Over There" to the repeated first lines of each of Huntington's four stanzas in the musical manner of the day, and soon this new gospel hymn was being sung far and wide by American believers and was being translated into a number of other languages as well.

After serving eleven pastoral appointments in the Genesee, Central New York, and East Genesee Conferences of the Methodist Church, as well as two terms as a presiding elder, DeWitt Clinton Huntington accepted an urgent call to serve the Trinity Church in Lincoln, Nebraska, against the advice and counsel of three Methodist bishops and many of his ministerial brethren. Bishop Andrew, who wanted to appoint Huntington to Rochester's First Methodist Church, told him that were he not his close personal friend he would refuse to transfer him to the Nebraska Conference. In 1891 Huntington and his family moved west, for he had remarried in Rochester in 1868, taking as his second wife Miss Frances H. Davis of that city. To their union, one daughter, her mother's namesake, had been born. For the ensuing five years, under the pastor's vigorous and inspiring leadership, Trinity Church in Lincoln, Nebraska, flourished. Large numbers of new members were added to the church, and a new sanctuary was built to accommodate the growing congregation in Nebraska's capital city.

After serving two terms as presiding elder of Nebraska Methodism's Beatrice District, the sixty-eight-year-old minister embarked upon the most important work of his long and busy life. The trustees of Nebraska Wesleyan University urged him to accept the chancellorship of the school, which was then about to close its doors due to embezzlement of funds on the part of a former trusted treasurer. On two occasions the aging pastor refused the position, accepting it the third time because, he said, the Lord had said to him, after he had prayed earnestly over the matter, "You are none too good to die under that pile of brick!" Under his dynamic leadership, the confidence of the church and the public in the college was restored, accumulated debts were paid off, and the university put on a solid foundation for future growth and expansion.

During all of those years, he continued to rise very early in the morning and devote regular hours to Bible study and private devotions. Between 1904 and 1911, he published several books and numerous sermons and addresses. He also represented his church in several of her general conferences in the United States, and in ecumenical conferences overseas. In 1908, several years after he had offered his first resignation to the trustees of the university, he was made chancellor emeritus and relieved of the heavy responsibilities of the educational institution, whose alumni continued to point him out as the man who had saved their school in her darkest hour.

Four years after his last retirement, the busy pastor died in his Lincoln, Nebraska, home on February 8, 1912, not long before his eighty-second birthday, passing "directly out of the activity of life to his heavenly home" which had long been his desire. He was buried in the Wyuka Cemetery in Nebraska's capital city. His last recorded words contained these revealing lines: "The Lord has saved my life three times when I was in imminent danger, and He has been in it all of the time when I was less conscious of it. I know He has been in every move of my life. It will be a joy to know what the next move is. It will be service somewhere, I am sure. There is no last—no chasm between this world and the next. My Heavenly Father is the same in any world; Jesus Christ is the same; surrender is the same; service is the same." In that spirit, Nebraska's "Grand Old Man" went forth to join "his friends over there" who, for so long a time, had been "watching and waiting" for his arrival.

THE HOME OVER THERE

D. W. C. Huntington.   Tullius C. O'Kane.

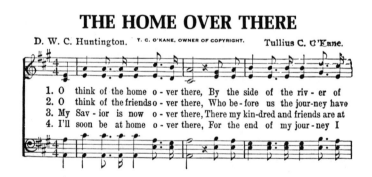

1. O think of the home o - ver there, By the side of the riv - er of
2. O think of the friends o - ver there, Who be - fore us the jour-ney have
3. My Sav - ior is now o - ver there, There my kin-dred and friends are at
4. I'll soon be at home o - ver there, For the end of my jour - ney I

The words and music of this gospel song are found in *The Cokesbury Worship Hymnal,* published in 1938 by The Methodist Publishing House, Nashville, Tennessee, Hymn Number 200.

50

6

Tell Mother I'll Be There

By the time ninety-two-year-old Rev. Charles M. Fill-more died in Indianapolis, Indiana, on September 18, 1952, his life had been inextricably interwoven with some of those who occupied the highest as well as the lowest positions in American society. In the span of half a century "a criminal and a king" had played their parts on the historical stage that was the United States, in both scenes of which this Christian minister became a participating actor rather than a bystanding spectator.

The "king" was none other than the popular President William McKinley, who, prior to his election to the nation's highest office, had served at various times as a lawyer, a congressman, and the governor of his native state of Ohio. Born of deeply devout parents, William was one of nine children. His consecrated Methodist mother, Nancy Allison McKinley, had early prophesied that her most promising son would make his mark in the world. "Some day," she often said, "William is going to be a bishop." When the talented lad chose to invest his life and influence in the political arena instead of in the spiritual, his mother was confident that he would act like the Christian gentleman he was reared to be in whatever profession he decided to play his particular part.

Those who knew that McKinley had been devoted to his church from earliest childhood and had served at various times as a Bible class teacher as well as a Sunday school superintendent, were not surprised when he slipped out of the executive mansion one day early in October, 1897, to make the train trip to Canton, Ohio, so he could walk to church with his mother and reminisce about the earlier days when she had taken her large family to Sunday school regularly week after week.

It was only natural that Mother Nancy, in her later years, leaned more heavily upon her husband's namesake than upon any of her other children, and no one was surprised when the president had her Ohio home connected with the White House by a special wire when she was finally bedridden with what was to be her last illness. In addition, the president ordered a special train to be held in readiness for a moment's departure should she take a sudden turn for the worse.

When the expected message came early in December of that same year, 1897, one of his aides whispered, "Mr. President, you'd better go." McKinley immediately wired back this brief, terse message, "Tell Mother I'll be there." He reached her side in time to hold her in his big strong arms as she breathed her last on Sunday afternoon, December 12, 1897. News of the telegraph messages that flashed back and forth between the humble Ohio home and the residence of the nation's "First Citizen" in Washington, D.C., reached the newspapers, and among those who read the account was Rev. Charles M. Fillmore. Immediately he said to himself, "There's a gospel message there."

Fillmore, a native of Paris, Illinois, where he was born on July 15, 1860, was the fifth of six sons born to pioneer preacher Rev. A. D. Fillmore and his wife. The father was a capable singer, musician, editor, publisher, and teacher as well. After taking his college training at Butler University, he entered the ministry of the Christian Church, the denomination whose life he was to enrich with his preaching and his music for the rest of his long, eventful, and fruitful years.

Charles, the fifth son, was the recipient of some of his father's musical and ministerial talents, and quite early tried his hand at writing stanzas and composing music. Soon he was mastering both crafts and creating new songs with almost effortless ease. One of the publications of the elder Fillmore, *The Christian Psalmist*, had proved quite popular, going through eighteen editions. This inspired Charles to follow the Scriptural injunction to "go and do thou likewise." His other brothers also took a cue from their father's successes and founded The Fillmore Brothers Music House in Cincinnati. One of them, James Fillmore, composed the tune for the familiar gospel song "The Beautiful Garden of Prayer."

President McKinley's telegram to Ohio, as reported in the newspapers, inspired Charles Fillmore to dash off a simple and singable new song which he entitled "Tell Mother I'll Be There." It began with these stanzas and chorus:

1. When I was but a little child how well I recollect
   How I would grieve my mother with my folly and neglect;
   And now that she has gone to heaven I miss her tender care;
   O Saviour, tell my mother I'll be there.

   CHORUS: Tell Mother I'll be there, in answer to her prayer,
   This message, blessed Saviour, to her bear.
   Tell Mother I'll be there heaven's joys
   with her to share;
   Yes, tell my darling mother I'll be there.

2. Though I was often wayward, she was always
    kind and good;
   So patient, gentle, loving when I acted rough and rude;
   My childhood griefs and trials she would gladly
    with me share;
   O Saviour, tell my mother I'll be there.

Rather than publish the song himself, Charles sold his four stanzas and chorus to his brother James for the handsome sum of five dollars, which, in that day, was above the average pay for what could prove to be a below-the-average musical success. For a few years James thought this was the case—until Charles M. Alexander, the song leader for the popular evangelist R. A. Torrey, found it in a gospel magazine. About three years after its first publication Alexander (of "The Glory Song" fame) sang it as a sacred solo for the first time at a meeting in Newton, Kansas. The poet-composer's own sister, Mrs. Cash M. Worth, played the piano accompaniment. The new number caught the church-going public's fancy and Charles Fillmore had the satisfaction of knowing that the four publishers who had rejected it before James purchased it had made a bad mistake.

After serving pastorates in several Disciples of Christ churches in Indiana, Utah, and Ohio, Rev. Charles M. Fillmore moved to Indianapolis in 1907 where he pastored several local congregations prior to his retirement in 1939. It was five years before he closed his last pastorate that Fillmore's path crossed that of "the criminal" —none other than the notorious gangster, bank robber, jail-breaker, and Public Enemy Number One, John Dillinger, Jr. After Dillinger had been relentlessly tracked down by the FBI, "betrayed" by his female companion, the much publicized "lady in red," and slain in a dingy Chicago alley, Rev. Charles Fillmore was asked to conduct the funeral services for him. His connection with the Dillinger family did not end there, however, for he later officiated at the wedding of the bandit's father, John Dillinger, Sr., and at the subsequent funeral of the stepmother as well.

In 1947 Charles observed the centennial of his preacher father's famous hymnal, and he himself continued to write and compose original hymns and songs until he had passed his ninetieth birthday. The last of his more than five hundred compositions, a song entitled "Christian Communion," was written in 1951, his ninety-first year. Ten years earlier, a newspaper story written on the occasion of his eightieth birthday contained this tribute, "The composer feels that with those two songs ["Tell Mother I'll Be There" and "Thank God for America," a patriotic hymn sung first for the Men's Bible Class of the Third Christian Church in Indianapolis, for which Fillmore played the piano for many years after his formal retirement from the active ministry], he has had a full life, even though there were hundreds in between. He says whenever he feels that he is getting old, he goes out to the back yard and weeds his garden or does a daily dozen on the woodpile and a home-made sawhorse."

Fillmore made his home at 5335 Washington Boulevard in Indianapolis for many years. After a serious illness of five months, he died in a north side nursing home in that city on September 18, 1952, at the age of ninety-two. Funeral services were held at Montgomery Funeral Home and burial took place in the Washington Park Cemetery. His wife, Maggie, had preceded him in death by two years, and the beloved nonagenarian was survived by two daughters, nine grandchildren, and nine great-grandchildren. Interestingly enough, the last two stanzas of his most popular song were in no way descriptive of the preacher-poet's own personal life, although they did describe the lives of many others who were numbered among "the wayward and the lost."

3. When I became a prodigal, and left the old roof-tree,
   She almost broke her loving heart in mourning after me;
   And day and night she prayed to God to keep
        me in his care:
   O Saviour, tell my mother I'll be there.

4. One day a message came to me, it bade me quickly come
   If I would see my mother ere the Saviour took her home;
   I promised her before she died, for heaven to prepare:
   O Saviour, tell my mother I'll be there.

TELL MOTHER I'LL BE THERE

C. M. F.

Charles M. Fillmore.
Arr. Geo. C. Stebbins.

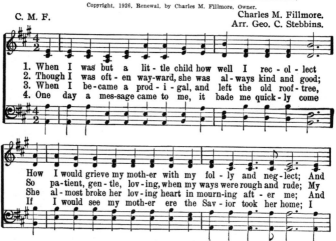

1. When I was but a lit-tle child how well I rec-ol-lect
2. Though I was oft-en way-ward, she was al-ways kind and good;
3. When I be-came a prod-i-gal, and left the old roof-tree,
4. One day a mes-sage came to me, it bade me quick-ly come

How I would grieve my moth-er with my fol-ly and neg-lect; And
So pa-tient, gen-tle, lov-ing, when my ways were rough and rude; My
She al-most broke her lov-ing heart in mourn-ing aft-er me; And
If I would see my moth-er ere the Sav-ior took her home; I

The words and music of "Tell Mother I'll Be There" may be found as Number 161 in the 1930 edition of *Seth Parker's Hymnal,* printed by Carl Fischer Inc. of New York City; it is also found as Number 146 in *Revival Hymns,* a Torrey-Alexander publication.

now that she has gone to heav'n I miss her ten - der care: O Sav-ior, tell my
childhood griefs and tri-als she would glad-ly with me share: O Sav-ior, tell my
day and night she prayed to God to keep me in His care: O Sav-ior, tell my
promised her, be - fore she died, for heav-en to pre-pare: O Sav-ior, tell my

Chorus.

moth-er I'll be there!...... Tell mother I'll be there in answer to her prayer;

I'll be there!

This message, bless-ed Savior, to her bear! Tell mother I'll be there, heav'n's

joys with her to share: Yes, tell my darling mother I'll be there!......

I'll be there!

7

The Glory Song

The first time that song-leader Charles McCallon Alexander (1867-1920) saw the song "O, That Will Be Glory for Me" in a new collection of gospel hymns and sacred songs, he hastily glanced over the words and music and then said to himself, "That man has wasted a page for I do not believe that song will be sung much." Even though the words and music had come from the prolific pen of one of America's most popular authors and composers of sacred music, Charles H. Gabriel (1856-1932), Charles Alexander tossed it aside, little dreaming that he was soon to be God's instrument for popularizing Gabriel's paean of praise and spreading its musical ministry to the far corners of the Christian world.

Gabriel grew up in a very humble home in Wilton, Iowa, where he had been born August 18, 1856, and early developed a great and abiding interest in music. His father often led groups of settlers in their evenings of singing, and those occasions awakened in the young lad a deep and lasting interest in religious hymns and sacred songs. He told his mother on one occasion that he was going to write a song one day that would become world famous, to which she replied, "My boy, I would rather have you write a song that will help somebody than see you president of the United States."

When the family finally purchased a small reed organ, Charles quickly mastered it and soon was not only playing and singing but also composing his own original songs as well, his first published composition coming from his pen when he was just fourteen years of age. Young Gabriel soon began conducting singing schools and leading choral conventions on his own, organizing and directing bands and glee clubs as well, his fame growing more rapidly than his income! On one occasion he supplied more than fifty new songs for a book that eventually sold more than one hundred thousand copies. All that the talented youth received from the unscrupulous publisher was a gift of one dozen free copies of the first edition! His later songs the accomplished musician sold for a dollar or two and when, on rare occasions, he received as much as two dollars and a half for an original manuscript, he thought he was almost as rich as Croesus!

George Sanville, the well-known music editor, author, and publisher, states that Charles Gabriel was inspired to write "The Glory Song" after hearing Mr. Ed Card, the superintendent of the Sunshine Rescue Mission in St. Louis, Missouri, punctuate his sermons with the word of exclamation, "Glory!" and close all of his earnest prayers with the phrase, "And that will be glory for me." These expressions became so much a part of the life and ministry of this remarkable man that his friends lovingly spoke of him as "Old Glory Face." In 1900, Gabriel, an established and successful composer of forty-four, poeticized Card's expressions, composing his own music to his original stanzas, the first stanza and chorus containing these lines:

1. When all my labors and trials are o'er,
   And I am safe on that beautiful shore;
   Just to be near the dear Lord I adore
   Will through the ages be glory for me.

CHORUS: O, that will be glory for me, Glory
        for me, glory for me;
        When by His grace I shall look on His face,
        That will be glory, be glory for me.

The new song was published that same year. A few months after thirty-three-year-old Charles M. Alexander had come to the conclusion that the song wasn't worth the paper it was printed on, he attended a large Sunday school convention and heard a huge audience singing "The Glory Song" with such contagious enthusiasm that he could not get it out of his heart and head for the next few weeks. It took such a deep and determined hold upon him that for days he could think of little else. Soon he was not only singing it himself, but teaching it to his friends and coworkers, all of them singing Gabriel's third stanza and chorus with gusto and grace:

3. Friends will be there I have loved long ago,
   Joy like a river around me will flow;
   Yet, just a smile from my Saviour, I know
   Will through the ages be glory for me.

Alexander confessed, "I dreamed about it and awoke to the rhythm of it." When he went with Evangelist R. A. Torrey to conduct a campaign in Australia, "The Glory Song" became the theme of their meetings, and soon the song-leader was surprised to hear telephone operators at their desks and hotel maids cleaning rooms, as well as workmen along the streets and business men in their offices humming and singing the stirring strains of the music of Charles Gabriel's gospel song. Before long "The Glory Song" was being translated into many languages, including Chinese, Dutch, German, Italian, Danish, Welsh, and even Zulu, and Alexander himself was receiving letters from people all over the Christian world attesting to the influence of that one gospel song upon their own individual spiritual lives.

In his subsequent evangelistic campaigns in the British Isles as well as in the leading metropolitan centers of his native United States, people spoke of Charles M. Alexander and "The Glory Song" as if they were one and the same. In fact, many people thought that the dynamic leader himself had actually written the stanzas and composed the stirring tune of the new sacred song, so closely was it then identified with his remarkable and inspiring musical ministry throughout the world.

No other composition from Gabriel's pen became as universally popular in so short a span of time as this one song, which eventually sold nearly twenty million copies, in twenty different languages. Although Gabriel himself wrote, edited, composed, collected, and published more than one hundred and fifty separate volumes of religious music during his lifetime, "The Glory Song" outsold them all. His other works included such familiar gospel tunes as "Since Jesus Came into My Heart," "He Lifted Me," "The Way of the Cross Leads Home," "He Is So Precious to Me," and such choral hymn anthems as "The Awakening Chorus" and "All Hail, Immanuel."

During the two score years during which he devoted all of his time and talents to the enrichment of church music, he composed more than eight thousand different tunes, his "Brighten the Corner Where You Are" and "Let a Little Sunshine In" being children's favorites for many decades. As editor for the Rodeheaver Music Publishing Company, he supervised publications that sold more millions of copies, writing and composing cantatas, oratorios, poems, and hymns and gospel songs with equal ease. A lifelong Methodist, Gabriel died at the home of his son in Los Angeles, California, on September 14, 1932. In 1940 he was elected posthumously to ASCAP (American Society of Composers, Authors, and Publishers) in recognition of his lasting contributions to American music.

As for Charles M. Alexander, he sang his way into millions of hearts and with his talented ministry of song he won thousands of converts for the Kingdom. He married a British girl, Miss Helen Cadbury, and made his home for some years in Great Britain, naming his English estate "Tennessee" after the state in which he had been born on October 24, 1867. He died very suddenly of a heart attack in his British residence on October 13, 1920, at the age of fifty-three, and was buried near the body of his infant son, their only child, at Lodge Hill Cemetery, Birmingham, England. On his tombstone are these words (the poem is actually the second of Gabriel's three stanzas for "The Glory Song"):

> Charles M. Alexander, II Timothy 2:15, Born at Meadow, Tennessee, USA, on October 24, 1867. Went home from "Tennessee," Moor Green Lake, Birmingham, on October 13, 1920.
>
> > "When by the gift of His infinite grace,
> > I am accorded in Heaven a place,
> > Just to be there and to look on His face
> > Will through the ages be glory for me."

The music which Charles Gabriel composed for these, his own words, in 1900 and which Charles Alexander had popularized, became so well loved in England that, when the Methodists of the British Isles prepared a new hymnal in 1933, the editors wedded the music of "The Glory Song" with some stanzas by Charles Silvester Horne

(1865-1914), making of them a new Christmas carol entitled "Sing We the King," Hymn 116.

As for "The Glory Song," its ministry continues to bless thousands of believers year after year who recall the labors of the two talented men and rejoice that their collaboration gave Christendom these joyous strains, by means of which untold millions have been able to voice their own praises and thanksgiving to God.

The words and music of this gospel hymn may be found in the 1928 edition of *The New Cokesbury Hymnal,* published by The Cokesbury Press, Nashville, Tennessee, Number 242. It is also Number 417 in *The Service Hymnal,* 1944 edition, published by Hope Publishing Company, Chicago, Illinois. While this volume lists Homer A. Rodeheaver as the owner, since he renewed the original 1900 copyright in 1928, the second period of twenty-eight years has elapsed and the song is now in the public domain.

O THAT WILL BE GLORY

Charles H. Gabriel

Charles H. Gabriel

1. When all my la-bors and tri-als are o'er, And I am safe on that
2. When, by the gift of His in-fi-nite grace, I am ac-cord-ed in
3. Friends will be there I have loved long a-go; Joy like a riv-er a-

beau-ti-ful shore, Just to be near the dear Lord I a-dore,
heav-en a place, Just to be there and to look on His face,
round me will flow; Yet, just a smile from my Sav-iour, I know,

ril..................... CHORUS *Faster*

Will through the a-ges be glo-ry for me.... O that will be
O .... that will

glo-ry for me, Glo-ry for me, glo-ry for me; When by His grace
be glo-ry for me, Glo-ry for me, glo-ry for me; ....

ril.

I shall look on His face, That will be glo-ry, be glo-ry for me.

8

The Saint's Sweet Home

The American actor and author John Howard Payne (1792-1852) was thirty years of age when he wrote the libretto for the opera "Clari, or The Maid of Milan" in Paris in October, 1822. "Clari" was actually a ballet that Payne was adapting for the English stage, but he little dreamed that his labors would one day inspire a British Baptist clergyman to pen his most popular hymn about heaven.

One particular tune that intrigued the young American had been composed by Henry Rowley Bishop (1786-1855) for a song that began "To the home of my childhood in sorrow I came." When composer Bishop suggested that he would like to use that tune to another set of stanzas in the forthcoming adaptation of his ballet, Payne searched for a theme that would be both worthy of the music and appropriate for the musicale for which it was intended. Then it was that, in a moment of loneliness and homesickness, the young man wrote himself into immortality with the verses that were later sung to Henry Bishop's lovely tune, when "Clari" was premiered in London's Covent Garden on the night of May

8, 1823, beginning his five original stanzas with these now familiar and nostalgic lines:

> 'Mid pleasures and palaces though we may roam,
> Be it ever so humble, there's no place like home!
> A charm from the sky seems to hallow us there,
> Which, seek through the world, is not met with elsewhere.
> Home, home, sweet, sweet home;
> There's no place like home, there's no place like home.

The song became an instantaneous success and soon was being sung, hummed and whistled throughout the British Isles. Ironically, the poet himself died at the age of sixty in Tunis, North Africa, many thousands of miles from his own beloved homeland and lay buried in foreign soil for thirty years, until, under the direction of the aged American philanthropist W. W. Corcoran, steps were taken for Payne's body to be disinterred from its North African grave and given a fitting burial in the soil of his own native United States, a venture that was climaxed on June 9, 1883, when the poet's body was returned to his own "home sweet home," being reburied with suitable honors in the presence of a distinguished audience in the Georgetown Cemetery, Washington, D.C.

The composer of the music to which Payne's stanzas are now universally sung was himself a native Londoner who gained well-deserved musical fame in England and was for a long time closely associated with Covent Garden as composer, conductor, and producer, being knighted in 1842, and receiving a doctor's degree in music from Oxford University eleven years later.

The widespread popularity of "Home, Sweet Home" caught the attention of Rev. David Denham (1791-1848), the son of a London clergyman who, at the age of fifteen, had been ordained to the Christian ministry, accepting as his first pastorate the spiritual oversight of the

69

Baptist congregation at Horsell Common. In 1816 young Denham moved to Plymouth and in 1826 to Margate, where he preached for the next eight years to the Baptists there. In 1834 he moved again and became the spiritual shepherd of the Baptists in Unicorn Yard, Tooley Street, Southwark, resigning only when ill health forced him to give up his extensive pastoral duties.

Following the relinquishing of his ministerial labors, Denham sojourned for a time at Cheltenham, Oxford, and then in Somerset, where he passed away at the age of fifty-seven, his final resting place being in London's Bunhil Fields Cemetery among many of Britain's noblest and greatest heroes and heroines, across the street from John Wesley's City Road Chapel, the mother church of world Methodism.

A prolific hymn writer, David Denham published a collection containing more than a thousand original hymns and songs in 1837 under the imposing title "The Saints' Melody, a New Selection of upwards of one thousand hymns, founded upon the doctrines of distinguishing grace, and adapted to every part of the Christian's experience and devotion in the ordinances of Christ."

It may have been during his pastorate at Margate (London) that Denham became familiar with Payne-Bishop's popular sentimental song, "Home, Sweet Home," which was still all the rage, and determined to Christianize it for his proposed hymnal, for Hymn Number 740 in this monumental publication is entitled "The Saints' Sweet Home," and contains six stanzas written in the eleven-syllable meter that Payne had utilized in his masterpiece, and perfectly adapted to be sung to Bishop's beautiful popular tune. Since using a well-known piece of music in order to popularize a Christian truth was as old as Martin Luther and the Protestant Reformation in

Germany in the sixteenth century, Denham did not hesitate to pen his poem with Bishop's melody in mind, and soon his people and the members of more than one hundred other London congregations were singing, to a well-known air, these new stanzas:

1. Mid scenes of confusion and creature complaints,
   How sweet to my soul is communion with saints;
   To find at the banquet of mercy there's room,
   And feel in the presence of Jesus at home!

CHORUS: Home, home, sweet, sweet home;
              Prepare me, dear Saviour, for heaven, my home.

2. Sweet bonds that unite all the children of peace,
   And thrice precious Jesus, whose love cannot cease;
   Though oft from thy presence in sadness I roam,
   I long to behold thee in glory at home.

3. While here in the valley of conflict I stay,
   O give me submission and strength as my day;
   In all my afflictions to thee would I come,
   Rejoicing in hope of my glorious home.

4. Whate'er thou deniest, O give me thy grace,
   The Spirit's true witness, and smiles of thy face;
   Indulge me with patience to wait at thy throne,
   And find even now a sweet foretaste of home.

Denham was on sound Scriptural ground in his hymn, for Ecclesiastes 12:5 contains this phrase with regard to frail man's final end, "Because man goeth to his long home," which has been variously translated "his long, long home," and "his eternal home," all of which means that, to true believers, heaven is not a church or a school, not a business establishment or a place of entertainment, not a bank or a stadium, not a secluded wooded spot or a store in the midst of humming commerce, but a home, with everything that that one word implies to both parents and children. King David, the "sweet singer of

Israel," had prophesied in Psalm 23, "And I shall dwell in the house of the Lord forever," while Jesus Himself had promised in John 14:2, "In my Father's house are many mansions." When love, therefore, abides within the walls of a house, that house becomes transformed into a home.

Rev. David Denham, named for Israel's noblest psalmist and singer, realized that his earthly home was but a foretaste of his heavenly home, and was prepared to recognize the heavenly because of his experience with the earthly. In that spirit he concluded his finest hymn with these stirring lines:

> 5. I long, dearest Lord, in thy beauties to shine;
>   No more as an exile in sorrow to pine;
>   But in thy fair image arise from the tomb,
>   With glorified millions to praise thee at home.

When the Methodist Church prepared the 1928 edition of *The New Cokesbury Hymnal,* Hymn 268 was "The Saints' Sweet Home," but it was titled merely "Sweet Home." Four of David Denham's five stanzas are included with Bishop's familiar music for John Howard Payne's song "Home, Sweet Home,"

'MID SCENES OF CONFUSION
AND CREATURE COMPLAINTS

Home 11. 11. 11. 11. wfth Refrain

REV. DAVID DENHAM, 1837

Ascribed to SIR HENRY R. BISHOP, 1823

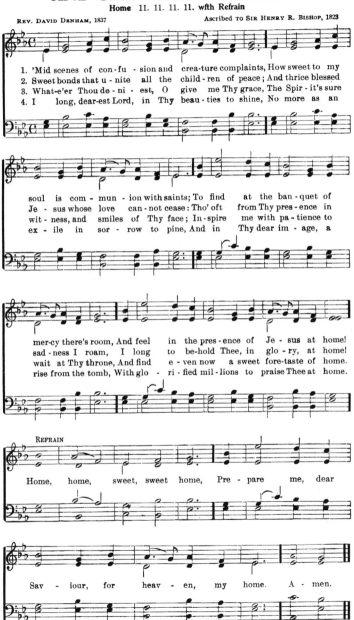

1. 'Mid scenes of con-fu - sion and crea-ture complaints, How sweet to my
2. Sweet bonds that u - nite all the child - ren of peace; And thrice blessed
3. What-e'er Thou de - ni - est, O give me Thy grace, The Spir - it's sure
4. I long, dear-est Lord, in Thy beau - ties to shine, No more as an

soul is com - mun - ion with saints; To find at the ban - quet of
Je - sus whose love can - not cease: Tho' oft from Thy pres - ence in
wit - ness, and smiles of Thy face; In - spire me with pa - tience to
ex - ile in sor - row to pine, And in Thy dear im - age, a

mer-cy there's room, And feel in the pres - ence of Je - sus at home!
sad - ness I roam, I long to be-hold Thee, in glo - ry, at home!
wait at Thy throne, And find e - ven now a sweet fore-taste of home.
rise from the tomb, With glo - ri - fied mil - lions to praise Thee at home.

REFRAIN

Home, home, sweet, sweet home, Pre - pare me, dear

Sav - iour, for heav - en, my home. A - men.

9

There Is a Happy Land

A melody by an unknown Hindu composer in India inspired a popular Sunday school teacher in Scotland to write a new poem, the result of their unwitting collaboration being a gospel song that became such a favorite with camp meeting congregations in the Deep South of the United States that most of the adults and children who sang it with contagious enthusiasm considered it another typically American religious folk song of unknown origin.

How the lilting little melody ever made the long journey from India to Scotland has never been determined, but one night when the Edinburgh head master, Andrew Young, was visiting in the home of Mr. and Mrs. Marshall, whose daughter was one of his pupils in the Niddry Street School, the young girl regaled her teacher by playing a delightful new piece of music on the piano, a selection which immediately caught the instructor's fancy. When he inquired as to its name and origin, all his host and hostess could tell him was that it was reputed to be of Indian birth and in its native land was familiarly known as "Happy Land." Mr. Young reasoned that more than likely a musical merchant-traveler, or possibly a

Christian missionary, had brought the music to Scotland from the faraway Orient land; but even at that, the actual composer could hardly have imagined that one of his finest original compositions would one day become a popular Sunday school hymn for Christian boys and girls in many countries of the globe far removed from the lands of the mystic East.

By the time Andrew Young had his sudden inspiration that memorable night in 1838, he had already proved himself an unusually capable instructor and teacher. More than likely he inherited these gifts from his distinguished father, David Young, who for more than half a century had conducted a training school in Edinburgh, where Andrew had been born on April 23, 1807. Following his early education, the young Scot had entered the university in his native city for a strenuous eight-year course of study in literary and theological subjects. When he was just twenty-three years of age, the Edinburgh Town Council was so impressed with his innate gifts as well as with his scholastic record that he was appointed head master of the school where he met young Miss Marshall for the first time.

The quality of his leadership and his ability to inspire those committed to his care is attested by the fact that when he took over the management of the school it had an enrollment of eighty pupils. When he left for another position ten years later, the enrollment had grown to more than six hundred students. It was two years prior to his severing his connection with Niddry Street to accept a better offer to serve as Head Master of Madras College, St. Andrew's University, that he was invited to the Marshall home.

After hearing the delightful and somewhat catchy tune played by his pupil, Young became so intrigued with it that he resolved then and there to write original English words which his own students could sing to the haunting air from far-off India. Taking as his subject matter the suggested title itself, "Happy Land," he immediately thought of the Christian view of heaven as just such a place deserving of such a name, and, almost before he knew what he was doing, he had written down three stanzas as unpretentious in their composition as the tune to which they were soon to be sung:

1. There is a happy land, Far, far away;
   Where saints in glory stand, Bright, bright as day.
   O, how they sweetly sing, "Worthy is our Saviour King";
   Loud let His praises ring, Praise, praise for aye.

2. Bright in that happy land Beams every eye;
   Kept by a Father's hand, Love cannot die.
   O, then to glory run; Be a crown and kingdom won;
   And bright above the sun Reign, reign for aye.

3. Come to that happy land, Come, come away;
   Why will ye doubting stand, Why still delay?
   O, we shall happy be, When, from sin and sorrow free,
   Lord, we shall live with Thee, Blest, blest for aye.

The children at the Niddry Street School sang the new stanzas so enthusiastically that when another Scottish clergyman and editor, Rev. James Gall, heard it, he resolved to include "There Is a Happy Land" in a forthcoming publication, *The Sacred Song Book*. So, five years after Young heard the music for the first time, Gall had it in the 1843 edition of his little collection of twenty-five new songs.

The book on which Gall collaborated with a local publisher, Robert Inglis, proved to be so popular that it was enlarged to include sixty selections and reissued in 1846. Eight years later it contained eighty songs, and eight years after that, in 1862, a hundred and thirty. By 1881, more than six million copies of these various editions had been printed and sold, and *The Sacred Song Book* had become the official hymn book for Sabbath schools in Scotland. In addition, "Happy Land" was soon translated by Christian missionaries into Chinese, Indian, and African languages and dialects, and converts old and new were joining their voices in singing the song that became Andrew Young's one claim to hymnic fame.

Young himself included the three stanzas in one of his own books published in 1876, *The Scottish Highlands and Other Poems,* but by that time the new song had leaped the broad expanse of the Atlantic Ocean and had been adopted by American Christians as well, few people asking any questions as to its origin and authorship, being content to accept it upon its own merits and make it their very own. Young proved as successful in heading the school at St. Andrew's University as he had in Edinburgh, and after thirteen years in that responsible position he retired and made his home thereafter in his native Edinburgh, serving for several years as the superintendent of the Greenside Parish Sabbath School in that growing metropolis.

Undoubtedly, staid and dignified Scotch Presbyterians would have been shocked if not absolutely horrified had they seen and heard hundreds of southern camp meeting folk in the new world clapping their hands and stamping their feet in rhythmic unity as they sang together Andrew Young's new song about heaven, adding, in the style of that day, many peculiar and original musical curlicues of their very own. But that is exactly what happened. "Happy Land" became such a favorite in the new world that it was included in many American song books and hymnals for several decades following its initial publication in Scotland in 1843.

Poet Andrew Young lived to celebrate his eighty-second birthday in his native city, and had the satisfaction of knowing, prior to his death on November 30, 1889, that his little song about heaven had literally sung its way around the Christian world and could be heard in every continent as well as in the weekday schools and Sabbath schools of his own beloved Scotland.

While many hymns on heaven have been written especially for children, or young people or adults, it is the general consensus that Andrew Young contributed one which proved to be not only one of the most universally popular but also one of the most appropriate for all ages and for all times. While he ranks as one of Scotland's finest minor poets in the anthologies of the day, on the rolls of popular authors of gospel songs he stands up there near the top with the most successful poets of Christendom, although he gave the church just one sacred song, when he was thirty-one years of age, the three stanzas of "Happy Land."

The words and music of this hymn about heaven may be found in *Hymns of the Ages,* edited by Robert P. Kerr and published in New York City by the A. D. F. Randolph Company in 1891. As Hymn 614, the author of the stanzas is listed as "Anon," while the tune, written in the key of E-flat, is named fittingly "Beulah," no composer's name being included with the music.

In *The Modern Hymnal,* published in Dallas, Texas, by Robert H. Coleman, and undated, it is Hymn 204. Again, no author's name is given, and the tune, designated merely as "Old Melody," is written in the key of D major.

HAPPY LAND

Old Melody.

1. There is a hap-py land, Far, far a-way, Where saints in glo - ry stand,
2. Bright, in that hap-py land, Beams ev - 'ry eye; Kept by a Father's hand,
3. Come to that hap-py land, Come, come a-way; Why will you doubting stand?

Bright, bright as day; Oh, how they sweet - ly sing, "Wor - thy is our
Love can - not die. Oh, then, to glo - ry run; Be a crown and
Why still de - lay? Oh, we shall hap - py be, When from sin and

Sav - ior King;" Loud let His prais - es ring, Praise, praise for aye!
king-dom won; And bright, a - bove the sun, Reign ev - er - more.
sor - row free, Lord, we shall dwell with Thee, Blest ev - er - more.

10

Heaven Is Here
Where Hymns of Gladness

The Rev. John Greenleaf Adams (1810-1887) was not only the sole Universalist clergyman to get a hymn in evangelical hymnals; he was also the only minister ever mistaken for a distinguished president of the United States. Because his middle initial was "G," some editors mistook it for a misprinted "Q" and credited his splendid hymn to President John Quincy Adams. "Quincy," as the president was familiarly known, a devout and dedicated Unitarian, did write several hymns before moving into the presidential mansion in Washington for a four-year stay in 1824, but he was not the prolific Universalist preacher, poet, and propagandist that "Greenleaf" was.

Universalism developed as a protest against the rigid, harsh, unyielding, and unbending doctrines of hyper-Calvinism (which even "out-Calvined" the great reformer himself) with its overly dogmatic descriptions of "the sovereignty of God" and its declarations about the fate of "unelected infants." George deBenneville, an English-educated French physician, began the movement with a series of sermons on "universal salvation" delivered during the middle of the eighteenth century in and around

Olney, Pennsylvania. John Murray, a chaplain in the Continental Army during the Revolutionary War, and Hosea Ballou, a school teacher from Vermont, took up the torch and spread this new doctrine far and wide.

Over against the five cardinal principles of Calvinism—total depravity, unconditional election, limited atonement, irresistible grace, perseverance of the saints (called the "tulip" truths since the five statements begin with the letters T-U-L-I-P)—the Universalists, after organizing themselves into a national body in Philadelphia in 1780, presented their five basic beliefs as follows: The universal fatherhood of God; the spiritual authority and leadership of His Son, Jesus Christ; the trustworthiness of the Bible as a revelation from God; the certainty of just retribution for sin; and the final harmony of all souls with God.

It took just a little more than one hundred years for these principles to be formulated to the satisfaction of every Universalist, and, although outlined in 1780, they were not fully and finally accepted until 1899. To these people, the basis for Christian fellowship lay in mutual faith and goodwill rather than in frozen formulas or classic creeds. Strangely enough, this very concept eventually became the creed of the creedless Universalists. While rejecting the idea that man is totally and thoroughly depraved, they accepted the contradictory idea that man is potentially good and even capable of perfection, probably failing to realize that the truth of the matter is that man is capable of both great sinfulness and great saintliness, the human heart being torn between the tugging forces that would raise man toward heaven or bend him toward hell!

To this religious group, John G. Adams, a native of Portsmouth, New Hampshire, gave his allegiance and to its ministry he was ordained. With others of this faith he pioneered for social betterment when crying needs for such reforms fell on deaf ears. In this way he and his coworkers labored to establish the kingdom of God on earth and sought to lay hold of a bit of its eternity in the midst of time.

Unlike the Calvinists who had tendency to "leave it all to God," the Universalists struggled and toiled as if God had "left it all to man," and rather than setting as their goal the personal attainment of heaven in life after death, they believed it was their bounden duty to bring heaven here on earth in their own lifetime.

"Heaven is both here and hereafter," Adams maintained, believing that life was both continuous and consistent, and that the life we live over on the other side of the grave would merely be a continuation of the one we lived on this side. "God is not inconsistent," the pastor stated. "He does not make a selfish man unselfish merely by the act of death. The unselfish person takes the same basic personality to the other country that he possesses in this world, for the fact of dying does not in any way alter one's essential nature or change one's ultimate character. So if you are seeking heaven, find it first of all in your own heart, and then labor and love and live to make it a reality right here on earth."

In this spirit, Adams sought to lift up the burdens of the fallen and to cheer the weary toiler along life's rugged way. Like his Master, he labored to free those who were "bound in the darksome prison-house of sin" and to share the anguish of the despondent and heavy-laden. Heeding the voice of duty with a smile on his lips and a song in his heart, he reflected the radiance of the kind of God he believed was his Heavenly Father. This universal concern for all mankind, and this assurance of the eventual salvation of each and every soul God had created for His own glory led the devout minister to practice what he preached in an unusually effective way.

In 1846 during the preparation of a new book, *Hymns for Christian Devotion,* on which Adams and a friend, Dr. E. H. Chapin, were working together as coeditors, the Universalist clergyman was inspired to write several hymns of his own, poems into which he poured his deepest personal convictions and disclosed his innermost feelings. Although King David in his most beautiful psalm had affirmed, "And I will dwell in the house of the Lord forever," Adams felt that heaven was here as well as there. He knew of the promise of Jesus to His disciples, "I go to prepare a place for you and if I go and prepare a place for you, I will come again and receive you unto myself, that where I am, there ye may be also" (John 14:2-3). The prophecies of John in the last book of the Bible, Revelation, pertaining to the "new heaven" were also familiar ones, but Adams still continued to believe that before anyone could inherit that Kingdom he had to prepare himself by helping build "the new earth" here below. With that in mind, he began his hymn with these words:

1. Heaven is here, where hymns of gladness
     Cheer the true believer's way,
   In this world where sin and sadness
     Often change to night our day.
   Heaven is here, where misery lightened
     Of its heavy load is seen,
   Where the face of sorrow brightened,
     By the deed of love hath been.

2. Where the sad, the poor, despairing,
     Are uplifted, cheered and blest,
   Where in others' labors sharing,
     We can find our surest rest;

> Where we heed the voice of duty,
> Tread the path that Jesus trod;
> This is heaven, its peace, its beauty,
> Radiant with the love of God.

Fifteen years after he wrote these stirring stanzas, Adams wrote another hymn for *Gospel Psalmist,* developing the same general theme, but suggesting that the songs of God's angels are not only heard up on high, but also down here below, when angelic deeds are performed by those possessing angelic hearts.

After his death in 1887, the editor of an evangelical hymnal altered Adams' original lines to make his hymn more acceptable to the general body of Christendom, and his first stanza now reads:

> Heaven is here, where hymns of gladness
> Cheer the toiler's rugged way;
> In this world where clouds of sadness
> Often change to night our day.

It is good that such a hymn has found a lasting place in our hymnals as well as in our hearts, for it is a constant reminder that only those inherit and inhabit the hereafter who have prepared and planned for it here.

In the 1935 edition of *The Methodist Hymnal,* this hymn is Number 461. It is sung to the tune "Austrian Hymn," composed as a national anthem by Haydn in 1797. Since the poem is written in 8.7.8.7.D. meter (in alternating lines of eight and seven syllables, with the pattern of four lines being doubled to make a poem of eight lines), the hymn may be sung to such familar tunes as "Love Divine" by Zundel, "Autumn" by Barthelemon, and "Hymn to Joy" by Beethoven.

HEAVEN IS HERE,
WHERE HYMNS OF GLADNESS

AUSTRIAN HYMN. 8. 7. 8. 7. D.

JOHN G. ADAMS, 1810–1887

FRANCIS J. HAYDN, 1732–1809

1. Heaven is here, where hymns of glad-ness Cheer the toil-ers' rug-ged way,
2. Where the sad, the poor, de - spair-ing, Are up - lift - ed, cheered, and blest,

In this world where clouds of sad-ness Oft - en change to night our day:
Where in oth - ers' la - bors shar-ing, We can find our sur - est rest;

Heaven is here, where mis-ery light-ened Of its heav - y load is seen,
Where we heed the voice of du - ty, Tread the path that Je - sus trod:

Where the face of sor-row bright-ened, By the deed of love hath been.
This is heaven, its peace, its beau-ty, Ra - diant with the love of God. A-MEN.

85

11

Brief Notes on Twenty Other Songs about Heaven

1. Beautiful Isle of Somewhere
2. Beulah Land
3. Beyond the Sunset
4. Crossing the Bar
5. Face to Face with Christ My Saviour
6. Good Night and Good Morning
7. Jerusalem the Golden
8. O Mother Dear Jerusalem
9. On Jordan's Stormy Banks I Stand
10. One Sweetly Solemn Thought
11. Pilgrim Stranger
12. Shall We Gather at the River?
13. Sunrise
14. The Holy City
15. The Home of the Soul
16. The Sweet By and By
17. There Is a Land of Pure Delight
18. When the Roll Is Called Up Yonder
19. When They Ring the Golden Bells for You and Me
20. Will There Be Any Stars in My Crown?

1. *Beautiful Isle of Somewhere*

Words by Mrs. Jessie Brown Pounds (1861-1921), wife of Rev. John E. Pounds, minister of Central Christian Church, Indianapolis, Indiana; written in 1897, soon after her marriage the previous year. She also wrote the stanzas of "The Way of the Cross Leads Home" and "The Touch of His Hand on Mine."

Music by John Sylvester Fearis (1867-1932) of "Little Sir Echo" fame.

2. *Beulah Land*

Words by New Jersey shipbuilder Edgar Page Stites (1836-1921) in 1875 while visiting the Methodist camp meeting grounds at Ocean Grove, New Jersey. He was a cousin of the Philadelphia poet Eliza E. Hewitt, author of "More About Jesus," "Sunshine in My Soul," and other sacred songs.

Music by John R. Sweney (1837-1899), a Pennsylvanian who was at different times a music professor, choral conductor, composer, and revival song leader. He also composed the tunes for Miss Hewitt's two hymns mentioned above.

This song is not to be confused with the gospel song "Dwelling in Beulah Land," written and composed by C. Austin Miles of "In the Garden" fame in 1911.

3. *Beyond the Sunset*

Words and music by Mr. and Mrs. Virgil P. Brock (Blanche Kerr), during the summer of 1936, while visiting at the Rodeheaver home in Winona Lake, Indiana; inspired by and hence dedicated to Horace and Grace Burr.

4. *Crossing the Bar*

Words by the British literary giant, Alfred Lord Tennyson (1809-1892); written in 1890 during the poet's eighty-first year. "His last poem was his best." Many musical settings have been made by various composers.

5. *Face to Face with Christ My Saviour*

Words by Mrs. Frank A. Breck of Portland, Oregon, a lifelong Presbyterian.

Music by the Methodist minister, Rev. Grant Colfax Tullar (1855-1934), in 1898 while staying at the Methodist parsonage in Rutherford, New Jersey. The tune was composed for the preacher's own stanzas "All for Me the Saviour Suffered," penned the night before he received Mrs. Breck's verses in the morning mail. The minister later became a partner in the New York City church music publishing firm of Tullar and Meredith.

This song is not to be confused with the sacred solo "Face to Face" which begins, "I know not now how soon 'twill be," with its chorus, "And I shall see Him face to face And be with those I love once more."

6. *Good Night and Good Morning*

Words by Mrs. Lizzie DeArmond, a teacher in the primary department of the Presbyterian church in Swathmore, Pennsylvania, written probably in 1912. She also penned the stanzas of "Mother's Prayers Have Followed Me" and "If Your Heart Keeps Right," for both of which songs B. D. Ackley composed the tunes.

Music by Homer Rodeheaver, song leader, composer, and music publisher, who sang this hymn at the poet's funeral.

7. *Jerusalem the Golden*

Words in Latin by Bernard of Cluny, between the years 1122 and 1156; translated into English by the British clergyman, poet, translator, and scholar, Rev. John Mason Neale (1818-1866) about 1861.

8. *O Mother Dear Jerusalem*

Original Latin stanzas by an unknown priest of the late sixteenth or early seventeenth century, known only by the initials F. B. P. Translated into English by the Scotch Presbyterian divine, Rev. David Dickson (1583-1663).

The tune "Materna" (the Latin word for "Mother"), to which "America the Beautiful" is now universally sung, was composed for this hymn by organist Samuel Augustus Ward (1847-1903) at Grace Church, Episcopal, in Newark, New Jersey, in 1882.

9. *On Jordan's Stormy Banks I Stand*

Words by the British Baptist minister Rev. Samuel Stennett (1727-1795), for the 1787 edition of Rippon's *Baptist Selection.* Stennett was joint pastor of London's Little Wild Street Baptist Church, Lincoln's Inn Fields, and the city's Seventh Day Baptist Church for many years. He also wrote "Majestic Sweetness" for the same edition of Rippon's book.

The music, with an original chorus added, was composed by R. M. McIntosh (1836-1899).

10. *One Sweetly Solemn Thought*

Words by Phoebe Cary (1824-1871) in New York City, in 1852. These stanzas, too, have had many different musical settings.

11. *Pilgrim Stranger*

This sacred song which begins, "I'm a pilgrim and I'm a stranger, I can tarry, I can tarry but a night," is said to have been the song that Abraham Lincoln heard Ann Rutledge sing as he was walking through the woods near New Salem, Illinois. When he recognized her singing voice as they worshiped in church the following Sunday morning, he turned and actually saw her for the first time.

The words came from the pen of a South Carolina native, Mary Stanley Palmer. Her first husband was Mr. Charles E. Dana, whom she married in 1835. After his death in 1839 she returned to her native state. In 1851 she married Rev. Robert D. Shindler of Kentucky. Hence, as a poet and hymn writer she is known by all three names. This particular poem first appeared in 1841 in the author's *Northern Harp*, a sequel to her successful *Southern Harp* of the previous year.

This song is not to be confused with another which contains a similar phrase. Rev. David Nelson (1793-1884), a rabid abolitionist, wrote some stanzas entitled "A Christian Psalm of Life" while hiding from hot-headed pursuers on the bank of the Mississippi River opposite Quincy, Illinois, in 1831. His opening stanza contained these words:

> My days are swiftly gliding by, And I, a pilgrim stranger,
> Would not detain them as they fly, Those hours
>   of toil and danger.

> CHORUS: For oh, we stand on Jordan's strand,
>   Our friends are passing over;
>   And just beyond the Shining Shore
>   We may almost discover.

The well-known author and composer of patriotic Civil War songs, George F. Root (1820-1895), was in his country home near North Reading, Massachusetts, in the summer of 1854 when his mother discovered Nelson's poem in a popular publication. She tore it out and handed it to her son with this comment, "George, I think that would be good for music." In a short while Root composed his simple tune for those stirring stanzas.

Rev. Samuel F. Smith, author of "America," paid this tribute to Root in a letter dated March 8, 1889: "It gives me unalloyed pleasure to speak a word in honor of the man whose genius has given to his countrymen and to the world the inspiring lays of 'Rally Round the Flag, Boys'; 'Tramp, Tramp, Tramp'; and 'Shining Shore.'" Although it is not as popular today, many people during the last half of the last century considered "Shining Shore" George F. Root's finest sacred song.

12. *Shall We Gather at the River*

Words and music by the Baptist clergyman Rev. Robert Lowry (1826-1899) in 1864, while serving as pastor of the Hanson Place Baptist Church, Brooklyn, New York, and originally entitled "Mutual Recognition in the Hereafter." It was written to comfort a bereaved member who had lost a child in death and has nothing whatsoever to do with the sacrament of baptism.

Lowry also wrote the words and music of "Where Is My Wandering Boy Tonight," and "Christ Arose," as well as the tunes for "I Need Thee Every Hour," "All the Way My Saviour Leads Me," "Marching to Zion," with an original chorus added to Rev. Isaac Watts' stanzas, and "Something for Thee," the latter being composed in 1871, the preacher's forty-fifth year.

13. *Sunrise*

Words by Methodist minister Rev. William Charles Poole (1875-1949), a member of the Wilmington Conference of the Methodist Church, in 1924. He also wrote the stanzas of "Just When I Need Him," 1908; "Did You Pray Till the Answer Came," 1915; "The Call of the Christ

Rings Out Today," 1914; and "The Church by the Side of the Road," 1925.

Music by Bentley D. Ackley (1872-1958), composer of more than thirty-five hundred hymn and gospel song tunes; the son of a Pennsylvania Methodist minister and brother of the preacher-poet-composer, Rev. A. H. Ackley.

14. *The Holy City*

Words by Frederick Edward Weatherly (1848-1929), a prominent British lawyer and poet.

Music by the English concert singer Michael Maybrick (1844-1913), who published many of his compositions under the pseudonym of Stephen Adams. Weatherly also wrote the stanzas of "Danny Boy" in 1910, two years before hearing "The Londonderry Air" to which they are now universally wedded; the popular World War I favorite "Roses of Picardy" in 1916; and several perennially popular sea songs and chanties. His autobiography, *Piano and Gown,* was published in England in 1926.

15. *The Home of the Soul*

Words by Mrs. Ellen Huntington Gates (1836-1920) in New York City in 1865. She also wrote the stanzas of "Your Mission," for which Sidney Grannis composed the tune, the song that became popular as President Lincoln's favorite hymn. She had penned those lines in 1860 at the age of twenty-five.

Music by Philip Phillips (1834-1920), the "Singing Pilgrim," also in 1865. It was Mr. Phillips' singing of "Your Mission" that caught Mr. Lincoln's attention. "The Home of the Soul" was sung at the composer's funeral in Fredonia, New York, by his close friend and fellow musician, Ira D. Sankey.

Boys Are Marching." He also composed several splendid sacred songs as well as the lilting music for the children's Sunday school favorite, "Jewels."

18. *When the Roll Is Called Up Yonder*

Words and music by Methodist layman James Milton Black (1856-1938), active leader in the Pine Street Methodist Church, Williamsport, Pennsylvania, in Williamsport in 1893. Mr. Black represented his church as one of the lay members of the committee that produced *The Methodist Hymnal* of 1905.

19. *When They Ring the Golden Bells for You and Me*

Words and music by Daniel A. (Dion) DeMarbelle (1818-1903), composer, soldier (G. A. R.), world traveler, professional circus clown, in 1887 while he was living in Kirkland, Illinois, during his sixty-ninth year. He died in Wayne, Illinois, and is buried in Bluff City cemetery.

20. *Will There Be Any Stars in My Crown?*

Words by Eliza Edmunds Hewitt (1851-1920), a Philadelphia Presbyterian, school teacher, Sunday school teacher, and children's department superintendent; part-time invalid. She also wrote "More About Jesus," "Stepping in the Light," "Give Me Thine Heart," and "There Is Sunshine in My Soul."

This song was inspired by Daniel 12:3, "They that be wise shall shine as the brightness of the firmament and they that turn many to righteousness as the stars for ever and ever"; and Revelation 12:1, "And upon her head was a crown of twelve stars."

Music by prolific Charles H. Gabriel (1856-1932).

16. *The Sweet By and By*

Written during the fall of 1867 in a drugstore in Elkhorn, Wisconsin. Words by druggist Samuel Fillmore Bennett (1836-1898).

Music by Joseph Philbrick Webster (1819-1875), who ten years earlier had composed the hauntingly beautiful melody of the love song "Lorena" in Madison, Indiana, for which a Universalist minister friend, Henry DeLaFayette Webster (1824-1896), no relation, had later penned the stanzas, creating the name "Lorena" to fit the composer's lovely music. This ballad became the most popular sentimental song of the Civil War era.

The gospel song was first sung by a male quartet composed of the poet, the composer, and two friends, S. E. Bright and N. H. Carswell, in the drugstore within an hour after it was written. When aged R. R. Crosby heard the men singing, he said, "That hymn is immortal."

17. *There Is a Land of Pure Delight*

Words by the distinguished Independent British preacher-poet, Rev. Isaac Watts (1674-1748), author of "Joy to the World," "O God Our Help in Ages Past," "Alas and Did My Saviour Bleed," "When I Survey the Wondrous Cross," and many others. Included in his collection *Hymns and Sacred Songs,* Book II, first published in 1707 under the caption, "A prospect of heaven makes death easy."

The tune "Varina," dated 1856, was from the prolific pen of George Frederick Root (1820-1895), the American musician and publisher who also wrote and composed some of the most popular patriotic songs of the Civil War era, including "The Battle Cry of Freedom," "The Vacant Chair," "There's Music in the Air," "Just Before the Battle, Mother," and "Tramp, Tramp, Tramp, The

Boys Are Marching." He also composed several splendid sacred songs as well as the lilting music for the children's Sunday school favorite, "Jewels."

18. *When the Roll Is Called Up Yonder*

Words and music by Methodist layman James Milton Black (1856-1938), active leader in the Pine Street Methodist Church, Williamsport, Pennsylvania, in Williamsport in 1893. Mr. Black represented his church as one of the lay members of the committee that produced *The Methodist Hymnal* of 1905.

19. *When They Ring the Golden Bells for You and Me*

Words and music by Daniel A. (Dion) DeMarbelle (1818-1903), composer, soldier (G. A. R.), world traveler, professional circus clown, in 1887 while he was living in Kirkland, Illinois, during his sixty-ninth year. He died in Wayne, Illinois, and is buried in Bluff City cemetery.

20. *Will There Be Any Stars in My Crown?*

Words by Eliza Edmunds Hewitt (1851-1920), a Philadelphia Presbyterian, school teacher, Sunday school teacher, and children's department superintendent; part-time invalid. She also wrote "More About Jesus," "Stepping in the Light," "Give Me Thine Heart," and "There Is Sunshine in My Soul."

This song was inspired by Daniel 12:3, "They that be wise shall shine as the brightness of the firmament and they that turn many to righteousness as the stars for ever and ever"; and Revelation 12:1, "And upon her head was a crown of twelve stars."

Music by prolific Charles H. Gabriel (1856-1932).